City Girl to Country Gal

*How a Farming
Community Accepted a
Young Girl's Family*

Anne Santin

ARCHWAY
PUBLISHING

Archway Publishing books may be ordered through booksellers or by contacting:

Archway Publishing
1663 Liberty Drive
Bloomington, IN 47403
www.archwaypublishing.com
1 (888) 242-5904

ISBN: 978-1-4808-7193-9 (sc)
ISBN: 978-1-4808-7194-6 (e)

Library of Congress Control Number: 2018964527

Print information available on the last page.

Archway Publishing rev. date: 04/22/2019

Dedication

I would like to dedicate this book to my dad, who passed away just before his ninety-second birthday. He was a kind, compassionate man with a great sense of humor. He always taught us not to take life too seriously and to enjoy every step we took in our lives.

All of us will miss you, Dad. I hope I make you proud with this story.

Contents

Opening

I didn't expect so many changes before the age of six. But as an adult looking back, that was one of the best parts of my life.

This is a short memoir of an experience I will cherish forever. I want to give my respect and admiration for farmers and how hard they work and how kind and helpful they were toward us city folk.

I wrote this as a story about a young girl's experience making the change from city life to country life, but it's my story.

I also wanted to write this for my parents. Thanks for my wonderful childhood.

I hope you enjoy.

Chapter 1

Our Move from City to Farm

My brother, sister, and I were born in a city in the southern part of the prairies in Canada. It was late 1960s, and it was one of the happiest times of my life.

Joe and I loved the city. We both had lots of friends within our little suburban neighborhood. On weekends, Joe and I would leave our house early on Saturday mornings, jump on our bikes, and head off in different directions to meet up with our friends. Emily was too young to be out on her own. These were the days when kids could disappear from their homes in the morning. We would hear one of the moms yell "Lunch!" and then we all knew it was time to go home for lunch. We would be off again for the afternoon on one of our adventures, until one of the moms yelled "Dinner!" and we all headed home.

Our summers were the best. There was a corner store in the neighborhood, and just across the street from the store was the city's outdoor swimming pool. During the summer, a couple times a week, we wrapped our bathing suits in our towels, met our friends at the corner store, bought a few candies, and headed off to the swimming pool. Many times our mom would let us have friends over for lunch (hot dogs and watermelon were the only things on Mom's menu), or set up our sprinkler and little blow-up pool. Our neighborhood was the best playground, and we loved it.

Dad had worked for an energy company since the early 1950s. His dad, my granddad, had passed away from a massive heart attack in his fifties, and my dad's first priority at that time was to take care of his sister and his mom. He started in the company mail room at the age of twenty and worked his way up to management. He loved his job, and we loved the company picnics and Christmas parties they hosted annually.

My mom would make Emily and I new outfits almost every Christmas. Mom was a great seamstress. We had red or deep-green velvet pantsuits or dresses. The company rented a part of the city playground for the picnics, with potato-sack races, tug-of-war competitions between the adults, and *lots* of food. After those picnics, we'd come home exhausted.

The school Joe and I attended was just two blocks away. When I started kindergarten, Joe promised my mom he would take care of me on the walk. With a wave goodbye to Mom, we headed down the hill to school.

Our mom had neighborhood friends, so there was no need to pack up Emily in the car for a playdate. There were plenty of kids Emily's age right in our neighborhood. Most of the neighbors were the same age as our parents.

Unfortunately, by the end of the 1960s, the economy was struggling. That was about to affect my family and change the world I knew and loved.

We lived in a beautiful four-bedroom home on a corner lot in one of the nicest neighborhoods in the city. We had a huge backyard. During the winter, Dad would make a skating rink. Almost every day after school, the neighborhood kids would drop their schoolbooks off at home, get their skates, come over to our house, skate till dusk, and head home for dinner. Our neighbors hung out in the yard during the summertime, too. Dad loved his patio and his barbecue grill. If Dad wasn't busy mowing the lawn or working in the garage, he would barbecue our hot dogs for lunch instead of Mom's usual way of boiling them in water.

The only request Dad and Mom made of our friends was manners. The kids coming into our home had to say hello, and thank Mom and Dad when leaving. If our parents greeted our friends first and there was no acknowledgment, our parents would take that friend aside and tell them that it was impolite (disrespectful) not to respond, especially if you were in another family's home. That was it. Other than that, our place was the cool, groovy place to hang out.

Halloween was my favorite time of year.

Mom was talented. She sewed, knitted, decorated, wallpapered, and so on. She made our Halloween costumes each year. In fact most of our clothes were sewn by Mom. Because it was the late 1960s, Mom made me the grooviest pair of jeans. She bought white denim material that was printed all over with peace signs and the words "peace" and "love." I loved those bell-bottom jeans. I would have worn them proudly to school every day if she'd let me.

It was the end of the summer of 1969 when we noticed something was happening. We didn't know what it was, but Dad and Mom's personalities were changing. There was a different atmosphere in our home. Dad was quiet and withdrawn or else constantly yelling at us. Before that, he'd never had a temper—ever. The rules had changed. Our friends were not allowed over as much as they had been in the past. Every once in a while, we'd hear Dad complain about feeding the neighborhood kids and say that it had to stop. We couldn't go to the corner store or the swimming pool or Saturday Matinee Theatre anymore.

Not only had the atmosphere changed in our

home, but there was a difference in the school and neighborhood. In the 1960s, parents rarely told their children what was happening in their lives. If there were changes, then the changes just happened—no discussion. Parents handled situations the only way they knew how, considering they had grown up during the Great Depression. To them, whatever life handed them as adults was not as difficult as their childhoods.

So, with no forewarning, we found out that our lives were going to change dramatically. Dad and Mom sat us down and told us that the company my dad worked for was in a financial crisis. Many employees had been fired, or "laid off" as we say today. Dad was one of the men laid off. The days we had thought Dad was going to work, he was actually looking for work.

When Joe and I walked home from school, we noticed "for sale" signs up on properties in our neighborhood. One day, we saw that sign on our lawn.

I ran straight up the driveway and into the

house, looking for Mom. I looked back at Joe. He had a defeated look on his face. I found Mom with Emily in the bedroom. There were empty boxes nearby. Mom was slowly pulling Emily's belongings from the closet and arranging them in the boxes. "What's going on, Mom?" I asked.

Mom didn't even look at me but kept packing. "Your father has found a new job, and we're moving. I've put boxes in your room. You need to start packing."

That was it. No warning. No explanation. Just "get packing."

I saw Joe enter the house and go straight into his room as if he were in a trance. He shut his bedroom door.

I had so many feelings: scared, sad, angry, confused. I didn't know what to do. I wanted to rip my room apart! Should I cry? Scream in anger? I felt so lost and disconnected from the world—my world.

Whatever new job Dad had, he was gone very early in the morning and came home late at night. This went on for a few months. One day when Joe and I were heading to school, the "for sale" sign had "price reduced" added to it. I didn't understand it, but my gut told me it wasn't good.

It was the last day at school for Joe and I, and we didn't know it. The whole school seemed quiet, like a forewarning. We walked home and arrived to see a big moving truck parked outside our home. All the neighbors were standing on our lawn and sidewalk. Joe and my friends were among them. Mom had organized a farewell gathering for us to say goodbye to our friends.

Mom was telling the parents of our friends that she'd keep in touch, and when we were settled, she would have our friends come and visit. Dad was talking to the movers, showing them a map of how to get to our new home. Joe and I just stared at our friends, and they just stared back. Joe finally made the first move and shook his friends' hands. I hugged my friends and tried not to cry. Emily might have been young, but she had picked up on the sadness and was crying.

That was that. We were gone out of the only place I had known as home.

Dad had sold our Oldsmobile and bought a used station wagon. Joe, Emily, and I silently rode out of our neighborhood, looking back at our friends. We sat in the back, facing backward, as our neighborhood slowly got smaller and smaller until it we could no longer see it.

When we'd left our neighborhood, we drove through a part of the downtown I remembered driving through every year to see the Christmas lights. I realized then we were leaving the city for good. Joe and I asked Mom and Dad where we were going. Mom said, "Your dad has found a job in a town outside the city, and we will be living on an acreage on the outskirts of the town."

Acreage? What was an acreage? It felt like a dream—a bad dream. Was this really happening?

From the main highway, we turned north onto a gravel road. Along the way, there were a few farmhouses. Farmhouses! Dad went by about four of them, and then he began to slow down as we approached a yard with a long driveway. We knew the house we saw at the end of it was our new home—or should I say "old" home? It was nothing like our beautiful home in the city.

Before we moved, the hippie era was already in full swing, and we seemed to fit in. But our experience was about to change drastically, considering the area we were moving into.

Chapter 2

Description of the Farm

The house we were moving into was owned by the Schmidt family. They had just built a new house across the main road and had sold their old house—to us! To me, it was ugly and old. To my mom and dad, it was a blank canvas. That was one gift we kids received from our parents: to be able to see the big picture beyond the mess.

There were huge oak trees surrounding the property, and a small area of dirt around the back of the house, suitable for a garden. The white fence around the house and yard needed repair, and the grass was patchy. The hedge that divided the front yard from the driveway either needed to be cut down or, by some miracle, just cleaned up.

When Mom and Dad married, they had built their first home. Later in life, they built other homes. But this was the first experience our family had with renovating an old house.

When we got out of the station wagon, Joe and I looked at each other and then just stared at the old two-story farmhouse. Emily held on to Mom's legs and wanted to go home. Dad told her this was our new home, and now we could get a puppy or maybe a kitten. Emily was hooked.

The house reminded me of houses I had seen in movies or on TV—for example, in *To Kill a Mockingbird* or *The Waltons*. The kitchen was a typical farmhouse kitchen. There was no dining room, just a large area in the kitchen where a huge table could be placed. There was one door leading to a sitting room and another door leading into a large living room that had three large windows looking out onto a veranda. There was a large workroom for Mom's sewing machine and all her crafts.

In the center of the house was a staircase that took us up to a small loft-style corridor that overlooked the living room. It led to three bedrooms, which meant Emily and I would have to share a room. I had loved having my own room in the city and wasn't impressed. Mom and Dad picked up on my attitude and ignored me—good idea. Of course Joe had his own room. At the end of the hallway was Mom and Dad's bedroom, and a bathroom that we would all have to share. This was very different from our home in the city. It was too much change, and I felt miserable.

Mom had four reasons why she loved this house: (1) the large kitchen; (2) the size of the garden she could make; (3) the large craft room; and 4) closets, closets, closets!

The basement was typical of an old farmhouse. It had been mostly used for storage and as a cold room. But my dad saw how he could make it a small but nice rec room. It took about three years for Dad to realize his vision would work. Eventually, there was a TV room, ping-pong/laundry room, cold room, and guest room (which later became Joe's bedroom).

Mom and Dad put in a lot of work on the acreage over the years. Even though my dad worked full-time in the city and my mom worked occasional temporary jobs, they loved working on creating their new home too. There were adjustments to make. Thank goodness for Mom's talents. She sewed curtains, painted trim, and wallpapered all the rooms. Mom knew how to reuse almost anything. Experts today who tell us how to recycle and reuse could learn a lesson from my mom.

Dad now worked for a small farm equipment and garden center. He could rent the equipment to fix up our yard at half price. With Joe's help, Dad repaired the grass and hedges and rototilled a new garden plot for Mom. They fixed the fence surrounding the house and planted more trees and shrubs. By the time our yard was finished, there were over one hundred trees planted. Along the driveway, the beat-up looking hedge produced small red roses that made it worth saving.

On the west side of the house, there was a large plot of grass that was quite patchy, but Dad repaired it and made it bigger. It became an area where we played lots of games: bad-minton, lawn darts, and football. Also on the west side of the house was a beautiful flower garden directly underneath the windows. Mom's magical skills brought that back to life.

Mom planted more flowers and shrubs in front of the veranda. Because of cost, it took about five years before the garden completely surrounded the veranda.

At the north end of the house was a large pussy willow tree that Emily and my bed-room window faced. On windy days, the top of the tree bent so far, it almost touched the ground. Mom cleaned up the debris under the tree and planted low-lying plants that needed very little sun. Every year when the tree blos-somed, Mom cut willows and made beautiful arrangements for our kitchen table.

This tree divided the backyard from Mom's mega-garden, which was beyond the fence and part of the farm field. That garden was the same square footage as our house. We had corn, potatoes, peas, tomatoes, carrots, herbs, rhubarb, strawberries, and raspberry bushes, along with many types of flowers. Every summer, we had to pick the potato bugs off the plants. Mom paid us a penny a bug. There were lots of potato plants, which meant lots of bugs. We made enough change to buy candy in town. Candy was a luxury, and we did not feel guilty about spending money we'd earned the hard way.

It took some time for me to adjust to starting a fresh, very different, new life on the acreage. There were no walks to the corner store or to the neighborhood swimming pool. But the quietness of living in the country was very peaceful. On the prairies, you could see the sun rise on the horizon in the east and set in the west. Watching it disappear is something I miss to this day.

Chapter 3

Our School, Inappropriate Dress, and My First Funeral

The part of the province where our acreage was located was populated by people of Dutch and German heritage. Most farmers were of Dutch Reform or Mennonite faith. In fact, all the farms surrounding our acreage were run by Mennonite farmers.

We were Catholics, city Catholics. There was a small population of Catholics in town, along with a few Catholic farm families There was one Catholic school that went from kinder-garten to grade nine, one public elementary school, one junior high school, and one senior high school in town.

On our first day of school, Mom drove us to

our new designated school, St. Peter's. She thought it best for us to learn our bus schedule and route from the school authorities, so she drove us in, and after school, we would be directed how to take the bus home.

When we arrived at the school, Mom came in with us to meet the principal and find out which classrooms Joe and I were assigned to. I was in grade four and Joe was in grade six. In the city, there had been two or three classrooms for each grade. In the country, there was only one class per grade.

We arrived just before the first period bell. As the kids started coming in from the school grounds, I felt I had stepped back in time. They looked like they had come out of the 1950s. I was reminded of my parents' family pictures. Joe and I looked at each other and then back at the kids, who were also staring at us.

Remember, we came from the city at the end of the hippie era. The young men in our city neighborhood would have fit in with San Francisco perfectly: long hair, headbands, suede coats with fringe. The hippie boys who had lived across the street from us walked with us to school, because the high school was next to the elementary school.

In our new surroundings, Joe and I looked like freaks. I was wearing my love-and-peace, bell-bottom jeans, and Joe wore striped bell-bottoms like the ones Mick Jagger wore strutting onstage.

The principal, Mr. Pineridge, and the vice principal, Sister Frances, welcomed my mom and us to our new school. Over the intercom, Sister Frances called Sister Mary down to the office to take us to our classrooms. I was dropped off first. As Joe was being led away, we gave each other a look of *oh boy*.

So there I was, standing at the front of the classroom, wearing my hippie pants, being introduced to my new classmates. Anyone who has been a new student in a new school knows what that feels like. But being the new student turned out better than I expected. All the girls talked to me right away and played with me at recess and ate with me at lunchtime.

Before the end of the day, the principal came over the intercom and asked Joe and I to come down to his office. All the kids in my class turned to me with terrified looks on their faces. I was embarrassed. I met Joe in the hall. As we walked, we shared our first-morning experiences with our classroom and class-mates. Joe had gone through much the same things with his grade six class as I had with my class.

When we arrived at the office, Sister Frances met us and asked us to sit down . Sister Frances was a nice vice principal. When Joe and I reminisce, we talk about how strict but fair Sister Frances was to all of her students. No matter what was said about a student, or how many times that student had gotten in trouble, each time they would receive a fair trial from Sister Frances. Many of the troubled kids found someone they could trust. It's not often you hear something positive about nuns or priests, understandably, but we lucked out.

Sister Frances asked us how everything was going. She asked if the other children were making us feel comfortable and if they had welcomed us. Joe and I nodded and told her that everyone had been very kind to us.

She proceeded to explain the dress code at the school. She talked about what young ladies and young men were expected to wear—and it was not hippie pants, vests, ponchos, or coats with fringe. In the city, we had fit in, but in this rural community, what we were wearing was not appropriate.

When we got home, we told Mom we were not allowed to dress the way we had done in the city. Mom and Dad could not have cared less that we had to dress in a more appropriate way because of the school rules. All they cared about were school marks—that was all.

Mom went through our clothes to divide what was appropriate for school from what we could wear on weekends. I was only in grade four, so this didn't bother me too much. I just wanted to fit in with the other kids and never be called down to the principal's office again.

As time went by, I started to fit in. It was about week three or four that I noticed there was one desk that was always empty. It was in the second row, the third desk down. I finally asked my new friend Kathy why there was an empty desk. Ever since I came to the school, that desk had always been empty. Kathy looked around to see if anyone was watching us and whispered, "That's Allison's desk. She's sick."

I didn't say anything. For the next few weeks, I watched to see if this Allison would come to school that day. Every day from my desk I sought a new face, hoping it would be Allison. I never met her, and it bothered me.

In the hallway of our school, there were the photographs from every year since the school first opened in the early 1960s. Each photo showed all the students at the school for each year, kindergarten through grade nine. The kindergarteners and grade one kids sat on benches in the front, and the kids from grades two through nine were in the back row. Whenever I got the chance, I looked for Allison. When I found my classmates in the photo from the year before, I looked for the face of a little girl I didn't recognize, in the hopes it might be Allison. Maybe she wasn't standing exactly with my class and somehow I missed her.

"That's her," Kathy whispered in my ear one day. I hadn't known Kathy was there. She had been standing by my shoulder. In fact, she had been watching me every time I stopped in front of the school pictures. She had figured out I was looking for Allison because I always stared at Allison's empty desk. "Allison was too sick for this year's picture. For last year's picture, she had to sit at the end of the bench with the kindergarten and grade one class, because she was too weak to stand."

I looked at the first row and saw Allison. I stared at her face for the longest time. She had long, curly black hair with a pink barrette on one side. She was wearing a pretty, pink, flowered dress, knee-high socks, and black shoes.

So now I knew what Allison looked like. Every day I still watched the classroom door, waiting to see the girl with the long, black curly hair come through our classroom door.

Unfortunately, I was never going to meet Allison.

One day our class was missing about five kids. My class was not big, so five missing kids was a lot. Sister Mary came in and announced that grades one, two, three, and four were going to the church, which was across from the school, to practice church songs and hymns. As we walked across the gravel parking lot, I asked another kid where Michael, Janet, Harold, Linda, and Daniel were and why we were going to practice songs and hymns in the middle of week. The kid told me it was for Allison's funeral.

I didn't know what to think or feel. I had never met her, but I missed her. Or was I just sad? I don't know. The five missing kids were Allison's close family friends and cousins.

I don't remember the hymns we sang the day of the funeral except for one song, "Make Me a Channel of Your Peace." Our choir sat in the balcony of the church, and from there I could see into the open coffin. The body lying there didn't look like Allison in the picture at school, but I knew it was her because of her hair and the pink bow. To me, she just looked asleep.

I don't remember the parents crying, or any of the other mourners. I just remember that Alison looked like she was sleeping.

Chapter 4

Our School Bus Rides

Going home from school, we learned fast that we were on our own with regard to catching the appropriate school bus. On the first day, Mom had thought that from our school, we would go straight to the high school, pick up the students there, and head home.

It turned out there were three buses for each school: St. Peter's (our school), D. McGrath Elementary School, and P. D. Harris Junior High School. The buses from our school and D. McGrath went to P. D. Harris to pick up the junior high students. All the kids got off the buses at the junior high school and re-boarded their designated buses. Those buses then headed to the high school to pick up the students there. After that, it was off to the farms. Some buses delivered kids to farms south of the town; other buses went north, east, and west.

The next day, all Mom asked of (or drilled into) Joe was to "watch over your little sister." I wasn't paying that much attention.

The next day, we did the bus routine ourselves. The morning routine was quite simple: we got on the bus at the end of our driveway and that was it. We'd see it coming down the main road from our bedroom windows, yell "Bus!" and head down the driveway. The bus dropped off the kids for the D. McGrath Elementary School first, our school second, P. D. Harris third, and the high school last. After school, it was more complicated. I put my faith in Joe to get us on the right bus again. Big mistake.

The first leg of the trip was from our school to the junior high. We made that part all right, but when we arrived at the junior high, I lost Joe. I didn't know which bus to switch to. I slowly walked from one bus to another, looking in the doors to see if I recognized the driver or any of the kids. I didn't recognize anyone, and I couldn't find Joe.

I was very scared, almost crying. I kept hoping I would see Joe somewhere amid all the other kids scrambling to get to their designated buses. I hoped to hear Joe's voice yelling for me over the chaos. Eventually I just stood in the middle of the parking lot, slowly turning, looking for Joe, holding my books and lunch box close to me.

Suddenly I felt a hand on my shoulder. I looked up and saw a tall young man. I recognized him from my bus ride that morning. He crouched down and said, "I think you're on my bus. Your family just moved into the house across the road from my aunt and uncle." He took my hand and led me to the bus.

As we got on, I recognized the bus driver. I climbed the stairs and saw Joe, already on the bus, talking to some of the kids from his class. He looked at me as if to say, "Oh! There you are … loser." I was so mad, I wanted to cry. But I never forgot the boy who helped me.

I found out he was a grade nine student who lived on the other side of our field.

Of course, when we got home, I gave Mom an earful about Joe. Then I headed upstairs to my bedroom. Joe gave me dirty looks after Mom had lectured him.

Over time, the bus ride home became my favorite part of the day. Our house was the third to last stop to be picked up in the morning and the third to last drop-off after school. Our bus ride home was about forty-five minutes long.

I loved looking out the bus window at the farms. Each season was so pretty. Because the city had many trees, I hadn't seen the big blue sky much there. It went on like an ocean outside the city. Whether it rained or snowed, eventually the blue sky would peek out from behind the clouds. It was beautiful to have that panoramic view.

In the winter, the snow was so white, it sparkled like it had tiny diamonds on top of it. When the sun shone, the fields were so bright from the reflection off the snow, I couldn't keep my eyes open. In the spring, I watched the combines preparing the fields. All the farms had beautiful gardens, and the yards were immaculate. I would see beautiful tulips, crocus, and iris beginning to peep above the snow. Most farms used these flowers as borders around gardens and along driveways. I loved to watch the trees begin to bloom. At first the branches looked like they were covered in a fog of green. Each day, the fog got thicker and darker until the tree had fully bloomed. My favorite trees were Mayday and apple trees. Their blossoms were picturesque against the plowed fields.

In this part of the prairies, only certain plants and vegetables could be planted in early spring, considering we could still get snow in May because spring was unreliable. One day it would be nice, and the next day I could wake up to snow on the ground. The vegetables that could be planted were potatoes, carrots, lettuce, and peas – these are the ones I remember because these are the veggies I still plant in my garden today.

By the time school was ending for the year,

everything was in full bloom. The rose bushes that lined our driveway were about to blossom into beautiful red buds. Everything was coming to life.

I don't think I could live in a place that didn't have four seasons. Each season is incredible to watch. Just before a summer thunderstorm, the dark clouds make the wheat fields look by neon yellow. After a rainstorm, the colors in the fields, trees, and yards were much brighter and seemed to glisten.

But my favorite season, even to this day, is fall. I love the warm colors on the trees and hedges, especially the ones that turn to a red/orange color. I could see foliage for miles—all the beautiful pops of orange and red from the trees, and the yellow wheat fields. There was so much going on in the fall. It was the start of a new school year and harvest. The main gravel roads were busy with combines and beet trucks getting ready for the harvest. Moms were out harvesting their gardens and preparing the soil for the winter.

Spring meant renewal for nature, but renewal

for me was fall. It was the excitement of seeing my friends again, with a promise to myself that I would do the best I could in school and always take care of my books and new clothes. Eventually I would have doodles all over my books and clothes all over the floor of my bedroom. Still, fall was and is my favorite time of year.

Chapter 5

Weather

Growing up on the prairies, the skies were panoramic—storms, sunrises, sunsets. Mom would say, "Red at night, sailors' delight; red in morning, sailors take warning." At the time I had no idea why she said that. We were on the prairies, not by an ocean, sea, or lake. But she was usually right.

When I went to school in the spring, I always wore a warm coat with mittens and a toque. I could arrive at school in the morning and the weather would be beautiful, yet by the time I left for home, it would be snowing. These storms could whip up winds in a minute. Spring was a very deceptive season—and many of us fell for its deception.

There was one storm that we remember and still laugh about today. The previous fall, Emily had started grade one. She was scared of riding the bus at first, but Joe and I eased her fears. Especially Joe—he was always very protective of Emily.

Mom had purchased spring jackets for Joe, Emily, and me. Joe didn't have to match, but Emily and I wore matching coats. Mom often dressed Emily and me in the same outfits when we were little, which didn't bother me. Many farm families didn't have a lot of money, and a mom would purchase enough material, when it was on sale, to make outfits for all their girls. The design of the dresses might be different, but all were made from the same material. Farm boys were always in jeans, because as soon as most of them got home, it was straight to the barn to help their dads.

Of course, matching outfits were big in the 1970s anyway. Husbands and wives or boyfriends and girlfriends would wear matching sweaters or coats. Sometimes brothers and sisters wore matching clothes. This is one part of the 1970s I hope never makes a comeback.

The spring jackets Mom bought for Emily and me reminded me of the spring coats Mary Tyler Moore wore on her TV show. The coats were red and hemmed just above our knees. They had big collars and wrap belts with white buckles. They were trimmed in white thread around the collar, hem, cuffs, and belt. All we needed were Nancy Sinatra's white boots. I loved my coat and thought Emily and I looked very modern.

The spring that year was different. We had had about three weeks of great weather. We begged Mom one morning to let us wear our spring coats to school, not the usual winter coats. We wanted to show off to our friends at school. Mom gave in, and off we went to catch the bus. It turned out that all the kids were in spring outfits. I guess a lot of moms got their arms twisted that day.

At morning recess time, we all headed outside to a dry playground. Normally during the spring, it was covered with water, mud puddles, and snow. The sky to the west looked dark, but we didn't care.

At our first recess, the winds were starting to pick up. Recess was in the gym, not outside.

Because our school included kindergarten through grade nine, the administrators had divided the gym into two sections: one for junior high kids and the other for grades one to six. The kindergarteners stayed in their classroom. It would have been overwhelming for them to play in the crowded gym.

Our gym did not have windows, so we had no idea what was happening outside. When the bell rang, the principal came into the gym and asked us to line up grade by grade and quickly head to our classrooms. As we left the gym, we looked out the huge entryway windows of the school and saw the heavy snow blowing up against the glass. A classic spring snowstorm had blown in.

Once we were back in our classrooms, the principal got on the intercom to let us know the school would be closing early and the buses for the farm kids were on their way. Town parents were called to pick their kids. The kids who lived close to the school just walked home. As the principal finished speaking, we saw the yellow buses pulling up. Our teacher told us to quickly pack our things.

The older students who had younger siblings in the school were told to get them from their classrooms and stand in the front foyer. Joe first came and got me; then we headed to Emily's classroom. After a head count by Sister Frances to make sure all the kids from each family were together, the town kids joined the farm kids in the foyer.

The principal got on the intercom again and told the farm kids to go to the buses. Moms from town were arriving to pick up their kids. The kids who lived close to the school ran home.

When the buses arrived at the junior high, all the kids got off and raced to their designated buses. It was chaotic. Kids were trying to cover themselves with their books, and the girls in particular tried to cover their legs against the wind-whipped snow. As the buses continued on to the high school, the skies grew even darker and the snow heavier. Visibility was getting worse.

Once the buses left the high school, it was every man for himself. The great thing about our bus drivers was that they were farm boys who had already graduated from high school. They primarily worked on their family farms and earned extra money by driving. These young men knew how to drive in bad weather.

The winds were blowing snow across the highway, creating almost whiteout conditions. You could barely see the road. The ditches and highway, covered in snow looked like one solid sheet of white. I have no idea how the bus drivers were able to drive.

After the bus had dropped us off, we ran up the driveway and noticed Mom's car was not there. Mom had left for her temporary job before we got on the school bus that morning. The house was locked up because Mom usually would have been home before us. Cell phones would have been so handy in those days.

Emily and I were cold and our legs hurt

because we were wearing skirts, knee-high socks, and our beautiful, *thin* spring jackets. Joe decided we should walk to the Wiebes's farm. He took his jacket off, wrapped it around Emily's legs, and picked her up. He turned to me and said, "Walk fast; Emily is freezing." My legs were so cold from the wind and snow that I couldn't feel them.

We headed up the road. I saw a huge figure coming toward us through the blowing snow. As it got closer, we recognized it was Mr. Wiebe. He had seen through the whiteout these two red "things" moving toward his house. When we were close enough, he recognized us and came running to retrieve us. He took his coat off and put it around Emily too. Then he, Joe, and I ran to his house. Mr. Wiebe, like the rest of our Mennonite neighbors, was a kind, sweet, and gentle man.

As fast as the storm had moved in, it was over. Because it was spring, the snow on the high-way was already melting by dinnertime. We saw Mom and Dad struggling to drive their city cars through the slush. We hopped into Mr. Wiebe's 4x4 truck, and he took us home.

Mrs. Wiebe called ahead to let Mom and Dad know we were on our way. Mr. Wiebe's truck plowed through the snowdrifts like they weren't even there.

We sat around the table that night, sharing stories of our day. We talked about the school bus trying to drive on the highway. Mom and Dad told us how everyone who lived outside of town had scrambled to get home.

The next day, over the town radio, we heard that schools were closed. Some of the farm roads had snow drifts as high as six feet. Joe, Emily, and I looked at each other and yelled, "Yay! No school!"

Not long after that storm, Dad sold his car and bought a used 4x4.

Chapter 6

Our Dog Bailey

Our family had never had an animal when we lived in the city—not a cat, dog, hamster, or goldfish. Growing up, Dad and Mom had had working farm dogs, but those had been outside dogs. They never came in the house.

We got our first puppy a short time after we moved to the acreage, a beautiful German shepherd. She was black with golden-colored paws and nose. We named her Bailey. She came to us in the late fall, almost wintertime. It was fun introducing her to our yard, her new playground. She just loved all the space where she could run and get in trouble. She sniffed everything! Her pattern was run, stop, bark; run, stop, bark. It was so much fun. Emily would be on the ground, laughing uncontrollably.

Bailey barked at the neighbor's cows and chased the neighbor's cats that were out for their daily explorations. When it first started to snow, it was funny to watch Bailey try to catch snowflakes. I had never seen a puppy do that. We'd throw snowballs and she'd try to catch those too.

By spring, she was getting quite big but was still a pup. She was always "inspecting" Mom's garden and trying to "help." If we were in the house, we sometimes would hear Mom yell, "Bailey! No! Emily, Joe, Janet! Get Bailey out of here!" We would call Bailey and she would run to us through the newly planted rows.

Because we only used about an acre for Mom's garden, a neighbor who lived two miles up the road harvested the alfalfa that grew on the rest of our land. They were the Bergens, and that spring, they met Bailey.

The Bergens had five kids: four boys and one girl. Their names were Jim, Ed, Cindy, Brian, and Albert. Cindy, being the only girl, was as tough as her brothers, and her brothers never pushed her around. Bailey loved her the most because when the Bergens would pet her, the boys sometimes teased Bailey, and Cindy would step in and push her brothers away. Of course, the boys *never* pushed Cindy back.

For the Bergens to get to the field to harvest, they had to drive through our yard. Bailey would bounce up to their vehicle, whether it was a truck or a combine, and give them a big welcome. The Bergen boys enjoyed our rambunctious puppy. The Bergens had two big black labs, but those dogs were trained to watch the Bergen homestead, not play. I think that's why the boys loved this new, bouncy puppy.

Emily and I had two friends that lived just past the Bergens' farm. Their names were Jody and Lori Neufeld. To visit each other, we rode our bikes back and forth to each others' farms. Emily and I learned to ride very, very fast. When it was our turn to visit Jody and Lori, Emily rode in front and I was right behind her. As soon as we got close to the Bergen farm, we geared down and picked up speed to get by ASAP. Usually, the Bergens' two black labs would see us and come running from the barn, barking. I would yell to Emily "Don't look back!" but she already knew that rule. I stayed behind Emily so that when the dogs reached us, they would get to my bike and not Emily's. Still pedalling, I'd yell and quickly kick out at the dogs. As soon as we passed the farm, they would stop chasing us and head back to their yard. I was never sure, but I believe that they would not have hurt us. They were just trying to scare us and protect their farm. The same thing would happen to Lori and Jody when they rode their bikes to our place.

This didn't happen all the time. Sometimes the dogs were in the field with the boys or in the back of the truck for a trip into town. It was a peaceful ride on those days.

Then we noticed that during recent visits to Lori and Jody's home, there had been no dogs. When we passed the Bergen farm, Mr. Bergen would wave at us. We'd see the dogs, and they barked, but they did not chase us. I told Lori that something weird had happened to the

Bergen's dogs. Lori said that their dad, Dan Neufeld, had called the Bergens. He told Mr. or Mrs. Bergen that when Lori, Jody, Emily, or I were planning on visiting each other, the dogs should be put in the barn or whatever—just not to let the dogs chase us.

Mr. Neufeld was a well-respected man in our area. He was also a *huge* man at six feet five inches in height. He towered over a lot of the farmers. If he hadn't been a farmer, he could have easily been a wrestler, though I'm not sure if there were Mennonite wrestlers at that time. He was a gentle man, but I would not have wanted to get on his bad side.

Alfalfa is harvested twice a year: first in the spring and then in September. When Bailey was a little pup, she would greet the Bergens before they went into our alfalfa field. She always stopped just at the edge that divided the field from our yard.

One day, during the second harvest, the Bergens came through our yard as usual. They stopped to greet Bailey, who was growing into a beautiful German shepherd. The

Bergens then headed into the field. This time, Bailey followed them.

I remember exactly where we were when Jim and Ed came running to the house. Dad and Joe were in the garage, Mom was in the sewing room, Emily was playing with her Barbies, and I was listening to ABBA in my bedroom. Emily and I heard the commotion in the house and went downstairs to investigate.

Mom came toward us, looking sick. She told us to stay in the house while she went outside. Emily and I went to the window. We saw Jim, Ed, Dad, and Joe running into the field toward the combine. Mom stood at the fence by the field. Joe came running back to the house. When he came through the door, I asked him what was going on. He looked at me and said, "Shut up!" I noticed he'd been crying.

He went to the phone, and I heard him talking with Mr. Wiebe but could not hear what was being said. Emily and I were scared. What had happened in the field? Had someone got hurt on the combine or by one of the trucks?

Joe left. I ran back to the window and looked down the field, but could only see the guys standing in a circle in the field looking down. Sometimes they were pacing. I then saw Mr. Wiebe running down the road toward our farm and he was carrying his shot gun. He ran into the field toward the men.

Emily and I were now terrified and ran down the stairs and out to Mom. "What's going on, Mom?" She hustled us back into the house and said Bailey had gone into the field while the Bergens were combining, and they did not see her in time. She'd jumped out from a crouching position right in front of the reel. Ed had seen her at the last second and tried to stop, but it was too late. All four of her legs got caught up in the combine and were mangled.

As soon as Mr. Wiebe reached the men, Dad and Joe came back to the house. Dad looked like he was ready to cry. He sat us down in the living room and explained again what had happened. They had to put Bailey out of her misery. As Dad was finishing that sentence, we heard the gunshot.

I had never saw my dad cry before that day. When you see your dad crumble into tears, it's a scary, helpless feeling. By then we were all crying.

When I am stressed or something traumatic happens, I have to remove myself. Back in the city, after Emily was born, Mom let Joe and I take Emily, who was six months old, for a walk in her stroller to the end of the street and back. We were both holding on to the carriage, and Mom was watching from the front step. There was a part of the sidewalk that had heaved up from the spring frost. Both Joe and I tripped over it, and we let go of the stroller. It went down the hill, hit a bump, and crashed at the side of the road. I freaked out and ran back home past Mom, who was racing toward the carriage. I hid in our garage. I was so scared that something terrible had happened to Emily, I did not want to come out. I had to know Emily was okay first. It took my parents and neighbors about an hour to find me.

So, after we heard the gunshot, I ran outside to my mom's garden and hid in the corn and cried. I don't know how long I was out there, but Mom and Emily finally found me. Emily's eyes were swollen and red.

I thank God for faith. Right there in the garden, Mom prayed for Bailey. She comforted us and told us Bailey was safe and pain-free, running in God's beautiful pasture.

It was our first hard lesson of farm life, and it wouldn't be the last.

Chapter 7

Our Cats and the Tomcat

It was close to the end of one of our summers, and we were getting ready to head back to school. Emily was going into grade one, I was going into grade five, and Joe was going into grade seven at St. Peter's.

The Bergens were again starting the second harvest of the alfalfa field. The haystack was right by the fence dividing Mom's garden from the field. The Bergens would come as they needed to pick up feed for their livestock.

The bales of alfalfa were stacked five feet high, three feet wide, and seven feet long. It was easy for kids to fall between the bales and suffocate, so we were not allowed to climb on them. But, being kids, we still did it, with the encouragement of Joe. We made sure Mom didn't see us.

Sometimes we would find baby mice. We would put them in the field and let nature take its course. Again, farm life is different from city life. Too bad we didn't know anyone who owned a snake.

One time when we were climbing the haystack, we realized something else had left its young. Joe knew the sounds he was hearing were not coming from baby mice, and as he crawled close, he found six kittens. They were so young that their eyes were not open yet.

We went and got Mom—and, of course, got in trouble for climbing the haystack. That aside, Mom said we should wait and not disturb the kittens, because the mother might come back. Mom was concerned though. How long should we wait? Where was the mother cat? Was she coming back?

The next morning, Mom did her usual morning routine of checking on her vegetable and flower gardens. Mom then went to the haystack, and as she walked around it, she found the body of what she believed was the mother cat. She knew it had been killed, but by what, she wasn't sure. She went to the garage, grabbed an empty box, placed a towel inside, climbed the haystack, and retrieved the kittens. Man, I would have loved to witness my mom climbing the haystack.

Mom brought the kittens to the house. One kitten fit perfectly in the palm of my hand. Mom asked me to come into town with her while Joe and Emily watch the kittens.

Mom and I went to the supermarket at the center of town, and then to the corner pharmacy. At the supermarket, Mom bought milk and Gerber rice cereal for babies. At the pharmacy, she bought eyedroppers.

When we got home, she warmed up the milk and added a little rice cereal so the mixture was runny. She then filled the eyedroppers with it, and all four of us, even Emily, fed the tiny kittens.

After we fed them, we put them on the towel in the box and kept them close to each other to stay warm. We kept this feeding ritual up until their eyes were open and they were crawling. Many times we took them out of the box and put them on a blanket so they would learn how to crawl and explore. Soon they were getting out of the box on their own. We then began teaching them to drink milk from a teacup saucer. As they grew, we took them to explore the outdoors.

We gave five of the kittens away, but we were allowed to keep one. Since farmers were always looking for more cats to kill mice on their property, Mom easily found neighboring farmers who wanted the kittens. Emily picked the kitten we kept. Her favorite kitten was completely black. There was a cartoon that Emily watched about a cat named Gracie, and that was what we named our first cat.

Gracie was a beautiful cat. Her coat always shone and she moved very gracefully. Her demeanor was quiet and loving. We believed that she was well liked among the male cats because there were always cats roaming near our yard.

When Gracie's first batch of kittens came

along, Mom and Dad were again able to give the litter away to farmers. It was what happened to her second batch of kittens that reminded us about animal life on farms.

The second litter contained four kittens, which we named Patches, Snowy, Buttons, and Tabs. Just like Gracie's first litter, they were kept outside until Mom could find farmers who needed them. Dad and Joe built a house for Gracie and her kittens. They filled it with old towels and covered the door with potato-sack material. The walls had a plastic lining on the inside to keep out the wind and cold. If it was really cold at night, Dad moved the kittens' house into the garage and left the door open a crack with a log.

That spring, the kids on the bus were talking about a tomcat that was roaming from farm to farm and killing other cats, especially kittens. This was one of the reasons why many farmers had more than one cat. Farmers lost cats to farm accidents or cars on the road or to predators, including other cats. Mom suspected that was what had happened to Gracie's mom.

The windows to Emily and my bedroom overlooked the back door and garage. We always had our windows open just a crack at night. One morning before Dad left for work, he went to the garage and then called out for Mom. We followed Mom out, only to be yelled at by Dad to get back in the house.

Every morning when we walked to the main road to catch the bus, the kittens would come and watch us leave. That morning, Joe turned to me and asked if I had seen Buttons. I looked over my shoulder and counted only three kittens. Where was Buttons?

After school, Emily went to play with the kittens. She noticed Buttons was missing. She went into the garden and garage looking for Buttons. Then Mom told us that Dad had found Buttons' body by the garage that morning. That's why he had told us to go in the house. If Emily had come out with us, Dad would have had to tell her about Buttons death, and it would have ruined her day at school.

Mom had also heard the rumors about the tomcat killing cats, and she believed that was what had happened to Buttons. She asked if I had heard anything unusual outside during the night. I hadn't, but I made sure I opened the window a little wider before I went to bed.

That night, I was awakened by the sound of a vicious fight happening outside. Anybody who has heard a cat fight knows it is the eeriest, creepiest sound. It's a sound you never forget for the rest of your life. I quietly got up and went into the kitchen, grabbed the broom, turned on the back porch light, and went out toward the garage. We didn't have the big farm lights that other farmers had, but I heard the growl and saw his eyes.

As I crept closer, I yelled, "Get out of here!" I held the broom over my shoulder like a baseball bat.

Those eyes belonged to a huge black cat. The size of him startled me. He had Tabs hanging in his mouth. I was not sad, upset, or scared—I was really angry! I yelled again at it, "*Get out of here!*" He dropped Tabs and crouched. I began swinging the broom. I hit the tomcat in the head but barely knocked him over. I kept swinging, kind of afraid he might lunge at me.

When I went to swing again, I felt someone grab the broom from behind. It was Joe. He'd heard me screaming—I was surprised Mom and Dad hadn't—and had come out with his baseball bat. Joe got one swing in before the tomcat stumbled and ran off like he was drunk. Joe was mad at me for being outside by myself and said that I should have come and got him.

Later that morning, as we were getting ready for school, Mom explained to Emily what had happened. Dad stayed home from work for a couple hours. We had a burial for Buttons and Tabs at the far end of Mom's garden. Emily wanted them buried together so they would not be alone.

Afterward, Dad drove Joe and me to school while Emily stayed home with Mom. On the drive, we got a scolding because we had gone outside without telling Mom and Dad. I didn't care. I would have done it again if that tomcat had come back. He never did.

Chapter 8

Learning to Drive

When I was in junior high, I thought it was time to learn to drive. Of course Joe was in high school and already driving, and my friends had their learners' permits. The boys in my class had already been driving their family trucks and combines in the field, and many of my friends were riding motorcycles at thirteen years of age. They drove through ditches, climbed the coulees, and raced each other. But the bikes were mostly used to set up irrigation pipes. I was itching to learn to drive.

Our lawn was now lush and encircled the house. Dad bought a riding lawnmower to keep up with our ever-expanding yard. He had already taught Joe how to use it, but Joe got a part-time job in town so Dad taught me. I wasn't the best at it, but my efforts still helped with the upkeep of the yard.

I told Dad I wanted to get my learner's permit, so could he teach me how to drive? It was springtime, and the farm supply store and garden center was extremely busy. Dad had been promoted to assistant manager and was too busy to teach me right then. When he wasn't working, he was repairing our deck or garage or house, or he was making a little time for the one extracurricular activity he loved—golf.

At Dad's former employer, there were many guys he worked with who would go golfing with him on a Saturday, or even sneak a game in during the week. My dad's company sponsored many golf tournaments to help kids in our local sports community. Unfortunately there were not many golfers on the farms, so Dad would call up his buddies from the city and golf as much as possible during the summer. My dad loved golf. When he was a young man, he almost became a professional golfer. The shelves in our house back in the city had been full of trophies he'd won since the late 1940s.

With Dad's time being so full, he recruited Joe to teach me. Joe and I thought it would be easy to teach me the basics on our long driveway, and eventually I'd graduate to the country roads.

So on a beautiful, warm, spring day, Joe and I headed out to the family car, a 1971 Chevrolet vehicle. Joe drove to the end of the drive-way and turned the car around. He put it in park, and then we switched seats. But before I was allowed to touch the steering wheel, Joe explained everything about how a car functioned. He showed me the brake pedal and the gas pedal. He explained what the letters on the gearshift stood for: *P* for park, *D* for drive, *N* for neutral, and *R* for reverse. He showed me the speedometer, headlights, turn signals, fuel gauge, and temperature indicator. In our car, to turn on the brights, the driver stepped on a silver button on the floor. He showed me that too. Blah, blah, blah!

At some time during this lecture, I zoned out.

I think it was around "*N* is for neutral." I didn't care; I just wanted to drive. I think I told Joe, "Shut up and let's go!"

Dad was working in the garage, Mom was doing something in the kitchen, and Emily was outside playing with a Barbie doll and the cats. On the south side of our driveway was the Wiebes' newly plowed field. Our properties were divided by a small ditch and barbed-wire fence. David Wiebe, the oldest son, was out in the field that day, preparing to plant the Wiebe's wheat crop. In fact, all the farmers around us were in the fields, readying the fields for crops.

Our car was an automatic, and the gearshift was on the steering column. Joe explained how to put the car in drive by pulling the gearshift toward me and then moving it up or down to the letter that represented what I wanted the car to do. After I put the car in "D for drive," Joe said, "Now take your foot off the brake pedal and lightly step on the gas pedal."

I did as Joe said and then pulled my foot off the gas pedal. Joe said, "You're an idiot! You have to keep your foot on the gas pedal at all times for the vehicle to move!"

I tried again, but the car barely moved.

Joe yelled, "Press the gas pedal!"

I yelled back, "I am! But you told me to press the gas pedal lightly!"

"Well, press harder!"

I didn't mean to, but I slammed my foot down on that stupid gas pedal. Next thing I knew, we were fishtailing down the gravel driveway. Joe shouted as I held on to the steering wheel for dear life. Everything happened so fast. I lost control, and the car flew over the ditch, through our neighbor's barbed-wire fence, and into his freshly plowed field—kind of like *The Dukes of Hazzard*. Joe lunged right beside me, kicking my foot away and slamming on the brake. Before Joe could yell "Get out!" I had the driver's door open and was running toward our house as fast as I could.

Unfortunately, Mom and Dad witnessed the whole thing. Mom was watching from the kitchen window, and Dad was on the ladder by the garage. As I jumped over the broken part of the barbed-wire fence, my stunned dad said something to the effect of "What the hell?" I babbled something back at him, out of breath, and went straight into the house.

Dad went to the fence and saw Joe driving our car out of the field, passing by an astonished-looking David Wiebe, who was still on the tractor. Joe drove the car through the Wiebe's yard and back home. I'm not sure, but as I was running back to the house, I think Joe waved and yelled to David, "Sorry!"

Joe drove the car back to our yard, got out, slammed the door, and yelled, "Janet!" My dad again asked what the hell had happened, but Joe was stomping his way toward the house. Of course I was in the house, hiding behind Mom. There was no point in going to my bedroom; there were no locks, and Joe would have burst through the bedroom door anyway.

When Joe got to the kitchen, Dad was right behind him, telling him to calm down. Joe kept yelling what an idiot I was and I should never be allowed to touch a car again. He even told Dad I shouldn't drive the riding lawnmower!

When he tried to get around Mom, I proclaimed, "It's your fault! You told me to step on the gas pedal harder!"

The yelling went back and forth until Mom declared, "That's enough! Both of you knock it off!"

Yikes! Had Mom just yelled at us? That shut both of us up.

Dad went outside to see if there was any damage to the car. Miraculously, there wasn't even a scratch. (Chevrolet makes great vehicles.)

Joe refused to have anything more to do with teaching me to drive ... ever! Dad signed me up for driving school. My driving teacher was nice *and* patient, and I did not fly over any more ditches.

Chapter 9

Getting Help from Our Patient Neighbors

Our property was surrounded by the properties of wonderful Mennonite farmers. South of us were the Bergmans and the Wiebes. To the north were the Janzen and Schmidt families. All of them were very kind, hardworking farmers. Looking back, I wonder what they thought of this Catholic city family moving into their territory. If they had any bad thoughts, they never conveyed them. As their faith instructed, they treated us as they would want to be treated.

Each spring, farmers burned the old grass in the ditches around their properties. This brought in new growth. Control burnings helped when the summers were dry and hot and old grass could catch fire more easily. After the ditches were burned, black was visible for miles on each side of the main road. Slowly, neon green popped through the black.. In the fall, farmers burned piles of leaves from their properties. Most farm properties had many trees surrounding the house and yard. Clearing was what kept the ground free of debris. There was less chance for accidental fires to get out of control.

I love the smell of burning leaves and grass. It's not very often this happens where I live now, but when I do smell burning leaves, it brings back great memories. Most of the trees that Mom, Dad, and Joe planted were at the west side of the house. They also surrounded Mom's garden. They divided the field from the yard, along with our fence. The trees formed a *U* shape, with the front of our yard open to our driveway. There were just two evergreens on the front lawn.

The Wiebes helped burn our ditches every spring. But one year, Dad and Mom decided that from now on, they would take care of their own spring burning. They meant to do this together, but because Joe, Emily, and I were off for Easter break, Mom attempted to do it with help from Emily and me. Dad went to work and had dropped Joe off at his part-time job.

Here is the lesson we learned: unless you've done a burning before and know exactly what to do, you should be supervised by a professional or a neighboring farmer.

We had shovels and rakes, and the hose was right beside the house. This seemed fool-proof. Our ditches were not that big, and that's why Mom thought we'd be fine doing it on our own. The ditch was supposed to burn south to north. Mom lit a match at the south side of the road, just at the start of our driveway.

The ditches were quite dry that year, and it didn't take long for the fire to ignite. Mom stayed close to the fire, holding a rake. Emily and I were just observers at that point. The wind had been a light breeze that morning but was slowly getting stronger. The flames flared higher and moved faster than Mom could keep under control.

We could always tell when our mom was angry or scared by the tone of her screams. The scream that came from Mom registered *terrified*. She yelled for Emily to bring the hose to her and for me to bring old buckets from the garage. Our buckets were empty ice cream pails.

Emily ran to the side of the house, turned the hose on, and ran back to Mom, who was trying to keep the flames away from our newly planted trees. Halfway to the flames, Emily was yanked to a stop. The hose was too short.

I came running out of the garage with three old ice cream pails. I saw what was happening and started to fill the pails from the hose. Emily raced to Mom, who was frantically trying to put the flames out.

Now, we had no idea how to put a grass fire out. We were doing it all wrong. We threw the water on the flames instead of in front of them. We should have been throwing water on the dry grass before the flames had reached it. Amateurs!

We ran back and forth with those stupid ice

cream pails full of water. I yelled at Emily, "Go in the house and pray in front of the picture of Jesus and Mary!" Mom told me to call the Wiebes for help, so I left her on her own. As I ran for the phone, I saw Emily praying in front of the picture of Mary. I dialed the Wiebes' number. Mrs. Wiebe had barely said hello before I was shouting, "Our farm is on fire and we need help!"

After I finished yelling at this person, who I *thought* was Mrs. Wiebe, a very kind voice, speaking German, said she had no idea what I was saying. I had dialed the wrong number.

The Wiebes lived about a quarter mile south of us. It turned out that Mr. Wiebe, David, and the Wiebes' younger son Brian had witnessed the crazy city family destroying their acreage. Before I could even redial, I saw the three Wiebes running toward our yard with shovels in their hands. They took over from Mom, and in a few moments all the flames were out.

Mom thanked Mr. Wiebe. He said his sons would help finish burning the ditch. I think the only reason Mr. Wiebe offered his sons to help us was because he was worried that we might burn ourselves up if we tried again.

Mom, Emily, and I stood there, covered in soot and water, our hair half in and out of our pigtails, holding the ice cream buckets, watching the Wiebe boys finish the spring burning project. Once they were finished, they waved to us and walked home.

When Dad got home, Mom told him everything. The responsibility for burning anything in or around our yard was officially taken away from us. The next day, Mom baked bread and oatmeal cookies to take to the Wiebes as a thank-you. The next spring, Dad and Joe took care of the ditches.

I'd like to give a shout-out to Jesus and Mother Mary for answering Emily's prayers by sending us the Wiebe family. Whew!

Chapter 10

Haunted House

When we first moved to our acreage, we did not know all the neighboring farm families. The lot south of us looked liked it had been abandoned. There was an old house that had probably been built in the 1910s or 1920s. I didn't know it at the time, but this was the Wiebes' property.

I loved it when my city friends visited me for sleepovers on weekends. I still missed my old home: hanging with my friends at the pool, riding our bikes around the neighborhood, and picking up candy at the confectionary store. Memories flooded back to me when my city friends came to visit.

My city friends also loved coming to our

acreage. It was such a different experience. We played lawn darts, croquet, and badminton. We had water fights, slept outside, and roasted marshmallows on the fire pit my dad had built during our first year there.

The first summer my friends came out to visit the farm, we would walk to the end of the field where there was a huge oak tree. There was a barbed-wire fence that divided our field from the farm field east of us. I loved that tree and my friends and myself sitting in it, talking about school and boys.

When my friends and I walked on the main gravel road, Dad made Joe walk with us. He was only two years older, but to us, he was ancient.

On one walk, a friend noticed the old abandoned house and asked about it. Joe told "his" story about the house's history—that it was haunted.

He said there had been a number of murders there about thirty years ago, and no one went on the property, since it was said to be haunted. He pointed to another house that was just east of the property and said that was where the Wiebe family lived. Mr. Wiebe and his two boys harvested the field around the abandoned house, but quickly left the property as soon as they finished. Joe said that besides the Wiebe family, no one went to the property. But sometimes at night, you could see a light, like a lantern, flicker for a few minutes in one of the windows on the second floor and then disappear.

That night in my bedroom, with my friends on the floor in their sleeping bags, we talked about wanting to get up early and check out the old house. I was mad at Joe for making up that crazy story, but I was also kind of excited. Now I had something even more exciting than a city pool or corner store to entertain my friends. I had a haunted house!

The next day was a dreary, windy Saturday morning. It was the perfect kind of day to check out the abandoned house. I told Mom we were going to one of our neighbors' homes farther south, so I could show my friends the Enns' newborn calf. That way we wouldn't have to bring Joe with us. Dad was always strict about Emily and me walking the main road when we first moved there, but Mom was a little more lenient.

So, with Dad out golfing for the day, we headed toward the abandoned house. As we started up its driveway, I was actually getting scared. Were the rumors true? Was Joe just being an idiot, hoping to scare little city girls? The wind blew through the branches of the huge old trees situated around the house. I started to question if this was such a good idea.

We noticed the front door was hanging on only a couple of hinges, something you wouldn't have noticed looking at it from my house or driving by. One of my friends, Susan, was more curious than scared. She yanked the door open. (She's probably some crime investigator or ghost hunter today.)

The inside of the house was something you'd see in those old horror movies with Vincent Price. Cobwebbed chairs were covered in white sheets. Broken windows made a ghostly whistling sound when the wind was blowing. The kitchen was to the left and some of the cupboard doors were hanging on by one or two hinges. More broken windows there had lace curtains flying like little ghosts in the wind.

The most eerie thing about it was that it looked as if the family had just up and left, leaving everything behind. It was frozen in time.

Susan walked through the house, picking up everything she could and examining it. My other friend and I stayed very close to one another. There were stairs going up to the bedrooms, but they were so damaged that there was no chance we were going to try climbing them. This disappointed Susan, the detective, but I was relieved.

We noticed there was a door at the side of the stairs. It was nailed shut with crisscrossing boards. Odd? I was beginning to believe Joe. I kept telling myself, *Janet, stop it!* and *I'm going kill Joe when I get home.*

There was another broken window on the first landing going upstairs. From that landing, the staircase turned left to the main landing on the second floor. The window on the landing had the same lace curtains as the kitchen, again flapping in the wind like a ghost.

We nervously giggled and were making jokes when we heard a bang in the kitchen. We looked at each other and tried to reassure ourselves that the wind must have blown something over. We looked up the stairs and again saw the curtains moving on the landing. But as we looked closer, we realized that window was *not* broken. There was not even a crack in it.

Without hesitation, we bolted from the house and ran down the driveway to the main gravel road and never even stopped until we were on my family's property. When we caught our breath, we saw my mom in the kitchen window. Joe was in the garage and Emily was in the backyard, playing with the cats. We killed ourselves laughing.

Before my friends' parents came to pick them up the next day, they kept teasing me, wondering if I was going to stay up that night to see if a light would shine in one of the windows. For the rest of their stay, my friends and I wouldn't even look at the abandoned house.

Later the same summer, Mr. Wiebe, David, and Brian pulled up in two pickup trucks and went into the abandoned house. They loaded furniture and belongings into the truck beds. It took a few trips to get everything they wanted with just two pickup trucks. The next day, a bulldozer tore down the old house. Then the land was cleaned up, and the Wiebes started building their new house.

We got to know the Wiebes. David and Brian's younger sister, Anna, became my friend. A few years later, I found out the true history of the abandoned house. Anna told me her dad had grown up there. Her grandfather had died in the 1950s, which left her dad and his brother (her uncle) to care for their mom and the farm. Unfortunately, her uncle was killed on that farm in an accident. The loss destroyed her grandmother, and she could no longer live in that house.

Anna said that her grandmother moved in

with them but did not want anything disturbed in the old house. You could see it perfectly from the house they were living in at the time. Her grandmother would sit by their living room window in her rocking chair and stare at the house every day. She passed away in the spring of the same year my friends and I explored the house. Mr. Wiebe and Anna's brothers cleared the house so they could build a new home and live on the property her dad had grown up on.

Once the new house was finished, Anna's mom created beautiful gardens and Mr. Wiebe planted more trees. It was like life had been restored on the abandoned lot.

And … maybe … .the curtains moving in the house the day my friends and I were there had been Mrs. Wiebe, visiting it for the last time.

Chapter 11

Vietnam Draft Dodgers?

It was the summer of 1971. In a couple of years, the Vietnam War would be declared over. I didn't understand the war, but eventually I learned more about it and how American boys who didn't want to fight in it came across the Canadian border to escape the draft. They were called draft dodgers.

I want to give you a little background about my mom and dad. In the city, Mom and Dad had been foster parents to two kids. I believe they were motivated to do this by what they had learned in their childhood. Both sets of grandparents always helped others out, especially when the Depression hit hard in the 1930s. Many families suffered, and my grandparents lent a hand when they could during that difficult time. My mom and dad likewise have always helped others out. They taught us to give to others less fortunate. Mom instilled in all of us the principle of being kind: "Do unto others as you would have done to you." My parents thought this was one of the most important rules in life.

In our farming community, you would see kids walking the main gravel road or riding their bikes or motorcycles. But you wouldn't often see adults walking the road unless they were the neighboring farmers. One time, though, two young men we didn't recognize walked down the road toward us. To me they were men but to mom they were boys because she thought they were about eighteen, if that.

Dad was at work and we were all outside when we saw them. My mom was at the end of the driveway, pruning her rosebushes. They came up to Mom and began talking to her. They carried huge backpacks on their backs. They had long hair tied back with bandannas around their heads. One had a beard; the other had a mustache. Mom spoke with them for a while, and then they went into our field. We saw them stop about a quarter of the way into the field. Mom came to us and told us that they were Americans on a camping trip. They had asked Mom if they could camp in our field for one night. They told Mom they were self-sufficient but needed a place to sleep. Mom said she had no problem with them camping, as long as they didn't light a campfire.

Again, this was about 1971. Young people were always hitchhiking across the country. I had older cousins who hitchhiked through Europe in the late 1960s and early 1970s. Those were different times.

When my dad arrived home from work, Joe and I watched him get out of his car, wanting to see if he would notice the two guys in the field. He did. He kept staring at the field as he shut his car door. Then he turned to us and asked, "Who's that?"

Joe and I just looked at each other, shrugged, and said, "Ask Mom."

Dad went inside, and we knew to stay outside. The only thing we heard was "You what?"

That was our cue to find something "useful" to do. Still, we tried to hear their talk in the kitchen. Dad's tone was irritated while Mom's was calm. One thing our parents never did was fight or yell at each other in front of us kids. I don't know how they did it. Dad's background was Scottish and Mom's was English and Irish.

We heard the back door open. We watched from the corners of our eyes as Dad walked into the field. Would he talk to these guys or just send them packing? They talked. After a few minutes, Dad shook their hands and came out of the field. Joe and I went over to him and asked what had happened. Dad kept walking. We kept at it: "What's going on, Dad? Did you kick them off? What happened?"

Without looking at us, he said, "They can stay one night, but they have to be gone tomorrow."

When I woke up the next morning, I looked down into the field, and the young Americans were gone.

When we talked about this years later, we all thought that they could have been draft dodgers. In one of my first jobs as a young adult in the city, I worked with a lady who had fled the States with her husband years earlier, so he could avoid being drafted. I don't know if this was true, but she said that her family and her husband's family were being monitored by the government. She said they could never go back home.

Chapter 12

Tobogganing and Other Winter Traditions

We had a few winter traditions on the farm that turned into the best times of our lives. One was roasting marshmallows on the natural gas fire pit at the center of our front yard. Others were skating on frozen ponds and canals surrounding the farms; tobogganing in the coulees; and, my favorite, tying our toboggan to the back of a 1961 Ford Mercury pickup truck and flying through the snow-covered fields. This was a truck Joe had bought for himself instead of using my parents' vehicles.

The coulees were the small, rolling hills you encountered as you headed into the Rockies—they were also called the foothills. In the area where we lived, some coulees looked like huge sand dunes with small bushes or trees sporadically growing on them.

In the summer, coulees were very popular with motorcyclists and ATV drivers. It was so much fun to watch drivers race up a coulee, hoping to get to the top before their machine toppled over. Onlookers would set up picnic lunches and watch these daredevils. It was a hot, crazy, fun event during the summers. For families, there were great spots for picnics and little hiking areas through the coulees. Sometimes after church, we'd go there. It was a nice way to end a weekend.

During the winter, the coulees were the greatest for tobogganing. Looking back now, I wouldn't have let my kids toboggan down a hill like we did—but again, those were different times. When our city friends came out to toboggan with us, Mom loaded up the station wagon with our sleighs, ski suits, thermoses of hot chocolate, and other treats, and off we went to enjoy a couple of hours of tobogganing.

I remember the magic carpet. It was a roll-up plastic sled that was popular when I was a kid. That's what our city friends used in the coulees. My family had an old-fashioned steel sled that could fit four or five small kids. It had a long string to pull it along, and rope handles along each side to hold on to while flying down the hill. If there were four of us on the sled, we'd listen to the kid at the front. This was usually Joe. He'd yell, "Lean left!" and we'd lean left. We missed the rocks and trees if we had the right person at the front of the toboggan. It was such a blast!

It took about half an hour to get to our favorite hill. There was no parking lot in the coulees, so Mom would park the car halfway in a ditch and halfway on the road. There was a little pathway to walk and then a small creek to cross to get to the tobogganing hill. Most coulees did not have much by way of trees or scrub, but you still had to pick the perfect spot so when you were flying down a hill, there were not many obstacles in the way.

When we arrived at the coulees, we'd get our snowsuits and boots on and pull the toboggan along the pathway, across the frozen creek and up to the top of the chosen hill. If kids want to get in shape, take them tobogganing into the coulees. The climb up was long and hard, but the ride down was worth it.

One year, we invited our old friends who had lived right next door to us in the city to come out and toboggan with us. The Anderson boys were fun and even nice to me, a girl! Kevin Anderson was Joe's good friend, and they stayed friends into their twenties. Scott was my age, and we got along pretty well. Joe had told Kevin about tobogganing, so Kevin and Scott begged their mom (Helen, a friend of our mom's) to let them go with us one Saturday. Mom and Helen had kept in touch over the years. When we lived in the city, Mom and Helen had always shopped together for bargains and borrowed from one another for things they needed, like ingredients for recipes.

It was a clear blue-sky Saturday morning when we headed to the coulees. It wasn't too cold—pleasant enough that we could spend a couple hours climbing up and flying down the hills. We loaded up the station wagons with toboggans, magic carpets, thermoses, and snacks. Emily and I invited our country neighbors Jody and Lori to join us for the trip.

Mom and Helen parked their station wagons half in and half out of the road. We all jumped out, put on our snow pants, snow coats, mitts, toques, and scarves, and headed toward the hill. Joe and Kevin were in charge of carrying the sleighs and helping Emily and Jody cross the creek. Mom and Helen stayed by the vehicles and used the backs of the station wagons as tables for the hot chocolate and treats we would devour after we'd finished tobogganing.

After Joe, Kevin, Emily, and Jody had crossed the creek, Scott, Lori, and I crossed. It was quite warm that day, but we had never had an issue crossing this small creek before. As the three of us crossed together, we heard a crack. We all froze and stared at each other. Joe and Kevin heard the crack and yelled, "Get moving, you idiots!" We attempted to take one more step—and the ice gave way.

It was a creek, so we couldn't be swept away, but there was enough water to completely soak us. As we crawled out onto dry land, we saw our moms running toward us. We knew the tobogganing trip was over. Joe, Kevin, and the girls had to find a way to cross back over the unbroken part of the creek to get to the cars.

The car ride home passed in complete silence. I have no idea what happened in Kevin and Scott's car, but Helen decided to go straight back to the city so Scott could get into some warm clothes. If Kevin treated Scott the way Joe treated me, I felt sorry for Scott. Emily and Jody were fine, but Lori was wet and cold like me.

We did manage other tobogganing trips with Kevin and Scott over the years, and they loved it.

Our other tobogganing tradition was more fun for Joe and our older cousin Brad: tying the toboggan to the back of Joe's truck and driving around our field. When our cousins came down for a visit in the winter, this was one of their favorite activities. Brad was a member of my uncle Tony's family. Tony was my mom's little brother. His wife was my aunt Maureen, and their kids were Brad, Gina, Dan, and Karen. Brad was around Joe's age, Gina was my age, and Dan was a year younger than Emily. Dan and Emily were close growing up and always looked out for each other. Then there was Karen, the baby. She was barely five years old. They would usually arrive at our house on a Friday night. We would have a big family dinner, watch some TV, and go off to bed, with our cousins sleeping on our bedroom floors in sleeping bags.

The next morning, all of us would be up very early. We ate breakfast, put on our snow gear, and headed outside. Joe and Brad would get the toboggan tied to the back of the truck, and then we would all jump in the truck for our morning toboggan race. Joe drove and Brad watched us through the back window. The rest of us jumped into the bed of the truck, among hay bales and blankets. This kept us warm as we waited for our turn on the toboggan.

The first to ride the toboggan were the little ones. With Karen being so small, Brad rode with his little sister. Joe was always very good at keeping the truck at a low speed. Karen wouldn't stay outside too long; that's why she was always first. Aunt Maureen would come out and get her after about a half hour.

Once Karen was gone, the rest of us did not want a slow and steady toboggan ride. We all loved hitting the bumps in the field and flying through the air. When the truck turned, often one person would fall off the toboggan and get lost in a dust of snow. We put our poor metal toboggan to the test for many winters.

One winter witnessed the demise of our trusty toboggan. The annual visit from our cousins was typical of past winters. They had arrived that Friday just before a snowstorm hit. Because of the storm, Dad wanted us to stay off the highways, which meant we couldn't drive out to the coulees. So it was settled: we would toboggan in the field and then drink hot chocolate and roast marshmallows at our fire pit. It was going to be a beautiful winter day.

The sky blazed blue, and we all had snow blindness for the first few minutes outside. Dad and Uncle Tony got in the bed of the pickup and set up the bales of hay and blankets. They helped Joe and Brad hook the rope up that pulled the toboggan. Dad and Uncle Tony lectured us, as always, about not standing up while the truck was moving. (Sometimes Gina and I would stand up, and our big brothers would yell in unison, "Sit down!")

Karen and Brad went first. Joe realized there were a lot of snowdrifts from the storm, so he took it especially easy with Karen. Instead of going back to the house, as she usually did, Karen climbed into the cab with Joe and Brad. This was much safer for her, considering how Joe drove when it was the older kids' turns.

The rule was once you were thrown from the toboggan, your turn was over. It was now Emily and Dan's turn. Joe would gradually go faster if Emily and Dan gave Brad the thumbs-up. Sometimes it was thumbs-down, but not very often. Brad asked Gina and I through the window what Emily and Dan wanted to do. As usual, they gave two thumbs-up, so Joe sped up. Emily and Dan held on for dear life. They flew over drifts and sometimes even through them. Finally, they were thrown from the toboggan. They slowly walked back to the truck, covered from head to toe in snow. They had to take their ski goggles off just to see the truck.

When it was Joe's turn, Brad drove and Joe and I were on the toboggan. When it was Brad's turn, he and Gina went with Joe driving. Finally it was Gina's and my turn. Joe was a good driver and was careful about how fast he went with Karen, Emily, and Dan. But how he drove for Gina and I was another story.

Gina and I noticed Joe and Brad talking to each other, looking back at us, and laughing. Two big brothers pulling their annoying teenage sisters on a toboggan tied to a truck? This should be interesting. What Gina and I didn't notice was the crack at the center of the toboggan. Joe started driving down the field, and Emily and Dan looked at us, watching for the thumbs-up or thumbs-down signal. Truth be told, rarely did our hand signals make much of a difference in how Joe drove.

The truck started out slowly, obviously to bug us. Brad said something to Emily and Dan. They laughed and yelled, "Too fast?"

We yelled, "No!" and gave two thumbs-up, but Joe barely sped up. Everybody in the truck was having a good laugh. Gina and I yelled, "Oh, come on! You guys are just being jerks!"

Emily yelled back, "So … faster?"

"Yeah!"

That was a big mistake. Joe took off so fast, the snow from the tires hit us and we had just enough time to grab the rope handles. At one point, I could barely see out of my ski goggles. As best as I could, I tried glancing back at Gina as we sailed over or through the snowdrifts. Her face was completely covered with snow. We could not do a thumbs-down because we were hanging on for dear life. I thought I saw Brad laughing his head off at us through the back window. I couldn't see any of the kids; they were probably crouched down in the bed.

As Joe took a corner, I squinted through my

goggles at a huge snow drift. Either we were going to fly over it or go through it. We flew over! Yay! I was so impressed that we had both held on—only to turn around and see half the toboggan gone and no Gina. When we hit that last snowdrift, the small crack grew into a large crack that split the toboggan in half.

I tried to get Joe to stop, but there was so much snow flying that I wasn't able to clearly signal him that we'd lost Gina. He finally turned around and saw only me on the toboggan. He brought the truck around, and we saw a lone person walking in the middle of the field, holding what looked like half a toboggan.

Joe was a very good driver, so, even though Gina startled him, he did not slam on the brakes and I did not go under the truck. He slowly came to a stop in front of Gina, standing there completely covered in snow. I got off and ran to the front of the truck to see Gina looking like Frosty the Snowgirl. We all stared at her—and then all of us burst out laughing.

Everyone got out of the truck, still laughing. Gina also laughed but also called Joe and Brad jerks. We brushed most of the snow off her, climbed back in the truck, and drove to the house. We piled the snow coats, pants, mitts, and boots in the mudroom as Mom announced, "I don't want to see a drop of water in the kitchen!" Then it was time for hot chocolate and marshmallows and another laugh at poor Gina's expense.

We did this cousins' tradition as often as possible growing up, and also did it with friends from town and from the city. Poor Mom and Dad would have been horrified if they had known all that happened in the field during our annual tobogganing events.

Chapter 13

Camping, Skiing, and the Black Widow

One of our favorite summer pastimes was camping. Mom and Dad had always enjoyed the outdoors, and our childhood vacations usually involved camping. We didn't have much money, and camping was a great, inexpensive way to see the country. We camped through Washington State, Montana, British Columbia, Alberta, and Saskatchewan.

We met up with our cousins on almost every trip and, as a group, traveled to different campgrounds for approximately two weeks every summer. We played musical cars with our cousins at every gas-station pit stop until we arrived at the next campground. Dad's vehicle was the favorite because it was a camper, and we would climb into the bunk area above the truck cab to look out the window.

Each family came in from a different direction, so Mom and Dad would set a meeting place. Once everyone had gathered there, it was off to the first campground on our adventure. We usually got to the campground in the late afternoon or early evening. As our parents and aunts and uncles set up camp, the kids explored the campground, the beach, and the forest trails. I don't know how Mom and Dad did it, but we always camped at the best campgrounds. There was lots of space between each campsite.

When we were younger, all we had to do was explore, but as we got older, we were given tasks to help set up. Joe's job was to get logs and light a campfire. Emily and I looked for branches for hot dog and marshmallow roasts. While exploring, we all had to find out where the showers and other amenities were and tell Mom and Dad. Dad put up the awning and chairs, and Mom started dinner. Our cousins were at the campsite right next to ours, setting up their tent trailer.

Mom was the second youngest in a family of seven kids. Sometimes her older sister's son, Darcy, would meet up with us with his friend Bill. They would stay a couple of nights; then off they would go in their 1970s mural-decorated van. We all thought they were cool until Darcy or Bill brought out their guitars. Darcy and Bill were huge country and western fans. I'm going to be honest: I did not enjoy 1970s country music. My parents loved Glenn Miller, Nat King Cole, Frank Sinatra, and Tony Bennett—music I still enjoy listening to today. But there we were, listening to Darcy and Bill play their favorite country songs.

The rest of the cousins would walk down to the beach, watch the sunset, and enjoy the quietness of the beach at night. Eventually the girls would end up talking about boys, at which point the boys would fake-gag and head to the other end of the beach. After the sun set, we'd get back to the campsite and roast marshmallows.

Every summer, our last camping trip was about a week before the start of school. That last trip was always in Montana, where we bought our school supplies and school clothes. Mom said that she could get great deals in the United States, much better than in Canada. Mom was a great bargain hunter. We had to be careful how much money we spent on clothes, so clothes shopping during the year was very rare. Each of us was allowed to pick out three new back-to-school outfits. Unfortunately, some of the clothes we wore were not *cool*. So at thirteen years of age, I got my first job, painting fences, and I was able to buy my first pair of jeans. This was the late 1970s, and by then *everyone* wore jeans. After that first paycheck, I didn't have to wear my brother's hand-me-downs.

Dad had relatives in the province next to us, but we didn't see them that much, especially in the winter, due to the road conditions. They came to our acreage once a year in the summer. Brad, Gina, Dan, and Karen lived only two hours from us; that's why we saw them more often. When our other cousins came to visit, we made the most of our time together because it was so rare. There were four kids in that family too: Jacqueline, Ronnie, Rachel, and Rebecca. They lived in one of the largest cities in that province and loved coming to our acreage. Uncle Ed could barely pull in before his kids would jump out of the car and start setting up their tent in our front yard.

Joe loved being in charge of setting up the tents with our cousin Ronnie. Ronnie was actually my age and Jacqueline was Joe's age. Ronnie idolized Joe and would do anything Joe asked him to do. Ronnie wasn't the most coordinated kid, but he was very eager to please Joe. I was impressed by Joe's patience with him. Hmm ... where had his patience been with me during that driving lesson? Oh yeah! I was the annoying younger sister.

My cousins on my dad's side were athletic and competitive—except Ronnie, who was more mechanically blessed. He now works for one of the largest airlines in the United States and is a top mechanic. But Jacqueline, Rachel, and Rebecca played baseball, basketball, soccer, and hockey, and you did not want to mess with them. Our family visited them one summer, and they introduced me to some of the neighborhood kids. When one of the kids shoved me off my bike, Rachel and Rebecca dropped their bikes, marched over to this kid, and got in his face, shoving him and telling him to back off and never do that again. He looked stunned. For the rest of our visit, he didn't come near me. I was actually kind of scared of Rachel and Rebecca, and I would *never* play any sports with them—just cheerlead on the sidelines.

Another favorite pastime was playing baseball in our recently harvested alfalfa field. Of course, there was no sliding into base unless you wanted to rip the skin off your legs. The older kids played with a real bat and baseball, but because Emily was the youngest, she was allowed to use a plastic ball and bat. She also didn't have to follow any rules. She could swing away until she hit the ball. Thankfully, she'd soon get bored and go play with the cats, which worked out because the other kids were itching to play a real baseball game. Dad and my uncle often joined in.

When my cousins became adults, they formed their own baseball team with my uncle as coach, and played in neighborhood tournaments. They got into fights all the time with each other, and we'd kind of back away if that started. Nevertheless, they are still very close today. They are all married with kids, but they hang out together and gather at my aunt and uncle's place on weekends

The Black Widow

What all our cousins and friends enjoyed the most was the Black Widow: a three-wheeler that we drove all over our field in the summer and fall. It had two huge wheels in the back and one small wheel in the front. It was completely black with two red stripes on the seat. There was only one seat but you could sit side by side to drive it. We entered it in the town's annual summer parade and used it to advertise new businesses, decorating it with the new store's signage and colors.

Joe usually controlled the Black Widow and would tease us when he was driving it. He pretended he was stopping to let someone else drive it, and then speed up again. We never wore helmets or padding for our elbows or knees. We just ripped around the field. Back then, we didn't wear seat belts in our car or truck either, and some farm kids would ride in the pickup bed.

Every summer when our cousins Brad, Gina, Dan, and Karen were visiting, we fought over who got to ride the three-wheeler. It was usually Gina and me fighting with Brad and Joe. But on one morning, Gina and I got up, dressed, and headed outside so we could ride the Black Widow before anyone else was up.

Unfortunately that morning, Karen and Emily were also up early, having breakfast. Thankfully, they were watching cartoons, so they were clueless about our plan. Mom and my aunt weren't clueless. They were in the kitchen and were perplexed why we were up so early. We told them we were going to the garden to get strawberries. I got the "what are you two up to?" look from Mom because I didn't like strawberries. Our moms worried about us riding the Black Widow without supervision. It was different for Joe and Brad. They were already driving so mom and dad didn't worry about them. But Gina and I knew, we'd be fine driving the Black Widow on our own. .

The problem was, when you started the Black Widow, it was loud. Gina and I knew Joe and Brad were going to hear us start it, so we devised a plan. We went to the garage, checked to make sure there was enough gas, and rolled the Black Widow into the field. Joe, Brad, and Dan were sleeping in the tent in the front yard. Gina was to keep an eye on the tent and give me a heads-up if anyone came out of the tent. She knew if we didn't get it started on the first try, Joe and Brad would grab the three-wheeler by the back cage that protected the motor, and there would be no ride for us that morning.

The first try, the starter failed. Second try, it started. Gina then yelled "Here they come!" I quickly looked over my shoulder and saw Joe and Brad running toward us, yelling for us to stop.

I yelled at Gina, "Get on!"

Joe just missed grabbing the cage and fell down. Brad jumped over him and also tried grabbing the cage. Too late! We were ripping through the field, laughing our heads off and seeing Brad and Joe in our dust. Yahoo!

We barreled down to the end of the field, turned around, and headed back toward the house. As we got closer, we saw Dan, Karen, and Emily standing by the fence. There was no sign of Joe and Brad. As we passed the three little ones, we saw our dads coming down the road. Gina saw Brad and Joe and yelled, "Snitches!" That didn't impress our dads.

We kept going, with Brad and Joe trying to catch us. We again went to the end of the field and did some figure eights. We approached the house and whizzed by the little ones, who were yelling at us to stop and let them have a turn. Gina's dad, Uncle Tony, chased us, trying to catch the back of the three-wheeler. After a couple of times buzzing by him, Gina and I looked at each other, laughing.

Suddenly we thought we hit a big bump that seemed to slow the Black Widow down. We couldn't remember hitting any bump before, so we just kept racing all over the field. As we looped by the house yet again, I noticed Uncle Tonywasn't there anymore. Mom and Aunt Barb were there, and they looked distressed. They were yelling at us, but we could not understand them. They pointed to the back of the three-wheeler, waving for us to look back. When Gina and I looked back, there was my uncle Tony holding on to the cage, not letting go until we stopped. There had been no bump in the field; it had been my uncle grabbing the back of the three-wheeler.

When we stopped, my uncle stood up, and his legs were bleeding and covered in multiple scratches. My mom and aunt were mad at Uncle Tony for grabbing on and not letting go, and then they laughed when they saw his legs. Uncle Tony was laughing too, but Gina and I were not laughing because we knew we were in trouble. Of course, we not only lost our privileges on the three-wheeler for the rest of the day, but for the rest of the time my cousins were visiting. On the day they were leaving, Gina and I had to take the little ones for a ride, and that was all we could do. Joe and Brad gloated and teased us at every opportunity for the rest of the weekend.

Skiing

Another outdoor activity Mom and Dad loved was skiing. If Dad had had his way, we would have camped while we skied. Thank goodness most campgrounds were closed for the season.

Our favorite ski resort was about two and a half hours from home. We skied four or five times during the winter months. The first time we skied, our mom and dad taught us how to snowplow, how to stop, and how to turn. In the late 1950s, just after Mom and Dad were married, they did a lot of skiing with my dad's sister and her husband, until they all started their families in the early 1960s.

Dad decided that a ski school might be the best way for us to become better skiers. It was a six-week course that met every Saturday. The meeting place was at a mall in the city. A Greyhound bus picked up the kids and took us to the mountains. This ski resort was closer to the city than the one we skied as a family. The age of the students ranged from grade three to grade twelve, and most of the kids were related. Joe, Emily, and I each had one friend who joined us, which made it much more fun than hanging out with a brother or sister.

So every Saturday for six weeks, we got up at five thirty and Dad or Mom drove us into the city to catch the seven o'clock bus. The seating on the bus was the same as our school bus: the smaller kids were in the front, the tweens in the middle, and the older teens in the back.

The older teens brought cassette tape and recorders. The girls Joe's age would sing along with the music, and sometimes we tweens would try to join in until we were told to shut up. Some of the guys in the back were so big, I thought they should be playing football or hockey, not skiing. I thought if they came racing down the ski hill and wiped out, someone would die.

When we arrived, our ski instructors were waiting for us just at the entrance of the ski chalet. They called out our names, and we gathered around to meet our teacher. Most of the kids in my age group were girls, though there were a couple of guys. We had lessons till noon, then lunch, and the afternoon was free ski until three thirty, when the hill started shutting down. We had to be back on the bus by four.

I remember a few Saturdays when it was -30 C (-22 F), and we still had our lessons. Our ski instructors made us do jumping jacks while we waited for our turn to show the instructor our progress. Yes! Jumping jacks on a hill in our skis! On those days, the lessons were usually cut short, and the chalet was packed with kids for the rest of the day with ski hills practically empty.

Most of the girls in my ski group were my age—the age of crushes on Donny Osmond, Tony DeFranco, David Cassidy, and the Bay City Rollers. Another hit at this time was *Star Wars*. It had come out the previous summer, and I loved that movie. I, like most of my friends, had a huge crush on Mark Hamill, who played a character named Luke Skywalker.

So when we saw our ski instructor, we stopped

dead in our tracks. Our ski instructor looked exactly like Luke Skywalker—I mean, Mark Hamill. Most of us couldn't remember what he was teaching or telling us to do because we were too busy staring at him. I think that's why we were the worst ski group on the hill that season. I'm not sure if he figured it out, but after each ski lesson, the girls from my group would race to the bathroom, fix our hair, and put on a fresh coat of lip gloss. We'd have our best-looking outfits on under our ski suits, just in case *Luke* came into the chalet during our lunch break. Having to get up on those Saturday mornings was not a problem for me and the other girls.

The bus ride home was completely different from the bus ride to the ski hill. Most kids slept, a few read, and there was no music. We were all wiped out from skiing. I'm sure the parents who picked up their kids loved it! Tired and quiet kids coming off the bus meant a peaceful Saturday night at home.

Chapter 14

High School

In the early 1970s, our town helped people trying to leave their war-torn or dictator-run countries to find better lives. Some had relatives overseas they were trying bring to Canada. The Vietnam War was coming to an end, and there were many Vietnamese families who still needed to get to a safe country. Our church sponsored families and helped them adjust to their new lives. I remember one family who had arrived from Vietnam had two small kids, and the dad, Bingh, now needed to find a job to support his young family. My dad helped Bingh find a job a the town's meat-packing plant. There were other men in the town who also worked at the meatpacking plant and would give Bingh a ride to work. I heard he was so excited, he would skip up to his fellow employees each morning. The other workers enjoyed such enthusiasm for work; they laughed at Bingh's keenness for the job.

There was another program my dad was a part of when we moved to the country. It was to sponsor people from poverty-ridden countries to visit Canada, learn more about agriculture, take what they learned back to their home countries, and implement it. There was one young man from Africa who came to stay with us for one summer. His name was Mosi. He came from Ghana, and he was about twenty-two years old. He was a kind and helpful young man. He helped Dad and Joe with all the yard work. He freed up Joe's time so Joe could work more hours in town. Mosi helped Mom care for her garden during the summer and plowed up more ground to expand it. He was so helpful that he would get upset with Joe and me (not so much at Emily) because he felt we were not helping our parents out as much as we should, especially with housework. He thought we took advantage of what we had and where we lived. He told us how blessed we were to be living in Canada.

So, gone were the days when we watched *Star Trek* every day—unless we had finished taking care of our responsibilities. It wasn't like we had a lot of programs to watch, considering we had only three channels. One station was for farming, one was sports and news, and one had programs we liked to watch: *Donny & Marie* (that was for me, not Joe), *The Carol Burnett Show*, *The Partridge Family*, *Star Trek*, and *Night Gallery*. It also had shows for Emily before she started school: *Mr. Dressup*, *Sesame Street*, and—her favorite—*Rupert the Bear*.

Of course, Mom and Dad were tickled pink with how much Mosi helped, but also with how he had us helping out more around the house and yard. So before Mom and Dad could assign us jobs, we made our own list. I took care of cleaning on Saturday mornings. My duties were cleaning bathrooms, vacuuming, dusting, and cleaning up the kitchen after our meals. Joe helped Mom with weeding, fixing appliances, maintaining the lawn mower, washing the vehicles, and picking up water to fill the underground tank that supplied the household water. Emily took care of cleaning her room, making sure the cats' house had clean towels, and putting the outdoor toys in the garage after use.

It made me feel proud when I saw the pleased look on Mom's face. One thing our parents taught us was to always be thankful when someone helped. The helper might not have done it the way you wanted it to be done, but nonetheless you should be grateful for their help. Mom complimented me on how well I cleaned the house. Dad was grateful that Joe was so handy with electrical and mechanical equipment. My dad never said to my mom, "That's your job," when it came to taking care of him and us. Dad respected what Mom did for the family.

I've carried that principle forward with my kids. When my youngest daughter was fourteen, she offered to mow the lawn while I was at work. I'd forgotten that it was a new lawn mower, and I hadn't yet raised the blade under the mower. She proudly showed me what she had done but said she couldn't get into the corners of the yard. She had mowed circles around the trees, and the rest of the yard was mowed in figure eights. Moreover, because the blade was so low, the grass was completely sheared off. I thanked her for her help and we had a good laugh. She'd done a good job, considering she'd never been taught how to mow a lawn. Our lawn survived and grew back to its beautiful glory.

While Mosi was staying with us, he met up with different farmers in our area to learn about agriculture. Dad was just responsible for sponsoring him. We weren't farmers. So Dad introduced Mosi to the farmers around town. Most of them welcomed Mosi and enjoyed showing him how they ran their farms.

But Dad made a comment out loud one time—not to anyone in particular, we were just outside in the front yard. Dad said, "When you are surrounded by white men and you bring in a person from a different race, you find out who is a racist and who isn't."

Dad had befriended one man in town when we first moved to the country. Sometimes Mom and Dad invited him and his family for barbecues at our place. Once Mosi came into the picture, Dad didn't have much to do with that man or his business. I always wondered if this former friend of Dad's was one of the people Dad was commenting about.

As usual, we went on our family camping trip that summer. Mom invited Mosi to come with us, but he said he had plans to meet with a few more farmers and would rather stay home and take care of the yard while we were away.

When we came back, Mosi met us at the door and was very happy to see us. But when we walked into the mudroom, we were allowed to go no further until we had removed our shoes—Mosi's orders. He even told Mom and Dad to remove their shoes. We hadn't unpacked the camper or lugged the gear into the house yet, which turned out to be a good thing. When we walked into the kitchen, the house looked like a show home. Everything sparkled! I though Mom was going to cry. He had cleaned all the windows inside and out, polished our floors, and dusted *everything*. I *never* dusted everything. The house looked gorgeous!

After Mosi left for Africa, I tried my best to keep it up the way he had, but I could never make it look the same way.

The next person to stay with us was an American exchange student. Lorraine was from Kansas. She and her girlfriend, Jennifer, decided to sign up for an exchange program through their high school. Lorraine came to Canada for one semester during her grade twelve year.

Her friend Jennifer was sponsored by a family in Whitehorse, Yukon Territories, and Lorraine came to our place on the prairies. I was starting grade ten which is the start of high school in Canada. Joe was in grade twelve like Lorraine, and Emily was starting grade six.

The misconceptions Americans had about Canada were quite amusing, especially in the 1970s. There was no internet, Twitter, or other social media to communicate information. We didn't have American stations on our TV because we didn't have cable, and I don't think Kansas got Canadian stations.

Lorraine arrived at the end of August and planned to stay through Christmas, heading back to Kansas in January for her second semester. Dad, Mom, Emily, and I went to pick her up at the airport, which was located in the south end of the city. Joe did not come along with us because he was putting in more hours at his job in town.

I was a little nervous for two reasons. First, she was going to share my room. The guest room in the basement had become Joe's room, and I had moved into Joe's old room. The second reason was the "what ifs": What if we don't get along? What if she's neat and objects to my messy habits?

Typical weather for us at the end of August was about 26 to 28 C (which is about 80 to 82 F). Canada measures temperature on the Celsius system. When Canada first switched over, Mom and Dad had to constantly look up the conversion from Fahrenheit to Celsius.

Unfortunately Lorraine had not been informed that Canada was on the Celsius system. So when she heard it was about 26 degrees, her friends and family told her that that was just how cold it was in Canada during the summers. She told us later that she almost backed out of coming up to Canada.

The airport was small. Passengers exited the planes onto the tarmac. We had no photo to go by, but Mom and Dad kind of figured out who Lorraine was when she got off the plane because she was in a khaki-colored parka with mittens and winter boots. It was an outfit you'd wear in the Arctic.

Lorraine was not very tall, and the parka seemed to envelop her. She had long, beautiful auburn hair that she struggled to keep out of her eyes as she was trying to carry her bag. I'm surprised now that no one on the plane said anything to her. The other passengers probably thought ... odd.

As all the other passengers walked past her, she slowly limped from the plane to the terminal. Mom and Dad waved at her, holding a sign with her name on it. Lorraine saw Emily and me and had a very puzzled look on her face. We, of course, were wearing shorts. Mom was in capri pants, and Dad was in his golf pants.

The first thing Lorraine said when she walked up to Mom and Dad was, "I was told it would be 26 degrees here."

Dad said, "Yes, in Celsius. That's about eighty degrees Fahrenheit."

Mom took Lorraine's parka and mittens. Underneath the parka, Lorraine wore a woolly turtleneck. It took all my parents' strength not to laugh out loud. Quick-thinking Mom asked Lorraine if she'd packed any clothes for the summer and our warm falls. Lorraine replied that she hadn't. So on our way from the airport, we stopped at Zellers to pick up some summer clothes for Lorraine.

It surprised us how shocked she was by the stores we had in Canada. "You have a McDonald's and Zellers and movie theaters!" she exclaimed. I gave her a side look, thinking, *What kind of kook is going to live with us and in my room?*

Lorraine did settle in, thank goodness. She

was very outgoing and loved living in the country. She said it reminded her of Kansas. She was surprised by the size of our high school. There were only two hundred students in total, compared to her high school back home that had over fifteen hundred students. But she enjoyed the smaller size of our school and met a lot of friends that she still keeps in touch with to this day. She learned to ski, loved our crazy toboggan rides behind the truck, and rode the Black Widow.

I love Facebook because that is how all of us keep in touch with Lorraine. I have posted old pictures of us from the 1970s. We all laugh at the pictures and tease each other about our cool clothes from the 1970s.

Chapter 15

Our Famous Grey Cup and Christmas Parties

The two events my parents were famous for were their Grey Cup and Christmas parties. In the winter, the surrounding farms reminded me of Christmas cards. There were Christmas lights on the houses, and some evergreens were decorated with lights too. They made the dark nights glow at Christmas.

Dad and Joe put lights on our house, the rosebushes that lined our driveway, and the evergreen tree at the front of the house. We had a huge living room window where Mom put the Christmas tree every year. By the time we got home from school, it was already dusk, and the first thing I would do is plug in all outside lights and the lights on the Christmas tree.

Our house was so beautifully decorated that Mom could have been a party decorator or had *Better Homes* magazine photograph our house. She received a lot of compliments, and each year she would add new touches to the house. When we held our annual Christmas party for neighbors and friends, Mom sought out a lot of appetizer ideas from different magazines. The food Mom prepared for Christmas was set up beautifully on our kitchen table. She used her best china, reserved for special occasions. There were red and green candles both large and small surrounding her handmade centerpiece.

Mom said I was a great help, but I knew deep down I could never meet her standards. Considering we were on a tight budget, she always pulled off her Christmas parties with class. When I have parties, I do it the lazy way—I buy appetizers at the grocery store. There is nothing made from scratch in my house.

There was plenty of room in the kitchen, basement, and living room for guests to mingle, but most people hung around the kitchen table. At the Christmas parties, Joe, Emily, and I were assigned duties. The guests found their own places to sit, and the three of us walked around with trays of food and made sure that everyone's plates were always full.

We had an upright piano between the kitchen area and the living room, and the adults who knew how to play would perform old-time Christmas songs, like the ones by Frank Sinatra, Tony Bennett, and Bing Crosby. At first maybe one or two people would be standing around the piano singing, and slowly, more people would gather. Then a couple of parents would rope their children into playing a few songs, which, of course, embarrassed the heck out of them, but you'd see their parents beaming with pride.

When we were younger, we went to Mass on Christmas Day. After we opened our presents, we'd get dressed while Dad went into the city to pick up our nana, Dad's mom. They came back, and we loaded up the station wagon and headed to church. Our family Christmas dinner was midafternoon, and then we relaxed the rest of the day by playing board or card games.

As we got older, the routine changed. We went to Midnight Mass, and after church we'd open our gifts while watching *A White Christmas* on TV. It always came on at about one o'clock in the morning. My favorite part of this new tradition was that we did not have to get up early, get dressed, and head into town for church. We relaxed and slowly prepared everything for an evening Christmas dinner. My parents also invited friends over whose kids had married and moved away, so they wouldn't be alone.

The magazines Mom read gave her great ideas for different events during the year: Halloween, Christmas, New Year's, Valentine's Day, Easter, Canada Day, and the Grey Cup.

In the United States, they have Super Bowl. In Canada, we have the Grey Cup, and the game is played just before the Christmas season. Canadians get as enthusiastic for the Grey Cup as Americans get about the Super Bowl.

Every year my mom and dad hosted their famous Grey Cup party, and our house was full of football fans. Of course we always cheered for the West, no matter who was playing.

The basement was the perfect place for Grey Cup parties. Our house was old, but it was spacious, and we could fill it to capacity. We had been living on the farm for about four years when Dad finished the basement. It held a ping-pong table, a sitting area for the TV, and a cast-iron woodstove. We loved being down in the basement, especially in the winter because of the woodstove. It actually kept the whole house warm. Also in the basement was the spare bedroom that Mosi stayed in and that Joe eventually moved into in his teens. Dad also built Mom a cold room. She made the best jams! When I got married, she gave me a list of everything I should store in my basement pantry.

For the Grey Cup parties, Dad would barbecue outdoors even though it was November. That didn't matter to Dad. He loved his barbecue! The grill was lit up right outside the back door. We didn't buy chips or treats during the year (couldn't afford it), but we did for our parties. There were always lots of desserts, chips, pretzels, pop, mixed nuts, burgers, ice cream, and homemade chili. It was heaven!.

Chapter 16

Leaving Our Home in the Country

Mom and Dad were now in their fifties and were getting tired of taking care of the large yard. After Dad had worked for a few years with the farming equipment company, the economy improved and he got a job with another energy company in the city. Mom got a part-time job working for the county. They eventually sold the farmhouse and found a nice house in a new subdivision in the city. Joe and I had already left home by then.

Joe moved farther west. He wanted to work for Parks Canada. He loved the mountains and joined the forestry department. He also wanted to be a volunteer firefighter. When he was in his early teens, there was a barn fire on the road just east of us. Joe and Dad went to help. He talked about it for weeks afterward, so I was not surprised by his career choice. He lives in the province next to us and has three great kids and one grandchild.

When I graduated high school, I went to college in the city. Most of my time was spent studying and working part-time. I was still living on the acreage and driving in and out of the city, so most of my money went toward gas. Mom and Dad had bought a new car a few years earlier and given the old one to us kids. Yes, the car I drove to college was the same car that flew over the ditch and through a barbed-wire fence. When I finished college, I moved into the city and started working for a law firm as a legal aide.

Emily was still attending the high school in the town when my parents sold the acreage. She wanted to graduate with the friends she had known since kindergarten. So Mom and Dad got a great deal through a family friend and bought a secondhand car for her to use. Mom and Dad knew it was only fair to let

Emily graduate with her friends, considering Joe and I had done the same thing.

It turned out that a couple of Emily's friends had farms close to the city, and they drove to the high school in the town. Emily met them en route in the country, and they would drive into the town together. Mom and Dad were relieved with this arrangement, especially in the winter. I don't know how parents did it back then with no cell phones. When your kids left the house, you just waited until they got home. You made sure they had change on them to call you from a pay phone if there was a problem, but other than that, you could only hope everything was okay.

Emily told me that in the fall, when the roads were still dry, she and her friends would race each other to their meeting place on the gravel roads, with each of them coming in from a different direction to see who would reach the spot first. That disturbed me, and I had to share with Emily what had happened when I was in high school. I was in grade ten and Emily was in grade six. She didn't remember what had happened.

That year, there had been two kids in grade eleven, a guy and girl. Their farms were close together on the other side of town, and they would race to see who could make it first to the main intersection. Everyone knew they did this, and other farm kids did the same thing. One day when these kids were again racing each other, they lost control and hit head-on, killing both of them instantly. They were barely seventeen.

I showed Emily my yearbook and a photo of the two kids. They had been popular and funny. Even the teachers had liked them.

I told Emily to stop. I was afraid she would keep doing this crazy stunt, so I also told Mom and Dad. They both had a talk with Emily, because Mom and Dad were acquaintances of the parents whose kids were killed. I asked Emily years later if she and her friends had stopped, and how long she had stayed mad at me for telling Mom and Dad. She said they raced only a few more times. The image of the kids kept creeping into her mind, though, and she and her friends finally stopped. She was quite angry with me for a while, but, as she put it, "I got over it."

Once Emily graduated from high school, she attended college in the city. She still had her country friends come to the city for sleepovers and shopping. Emily and I became best friends. She was my maid of honor and I was her matron of honor. Unfortunately, Emily's husband got a job in California, and they moved there a long time ago. They have two great kids now in college. We all visit Emily and Doug frequently, and they come back to Canada as much as possible. Of course they have so many Canadian friends and family coming to visit, they don't need to come back home to see everyone. That's what you get for moving to a beautiful, warm part of America.

When we all get together, we look back fondly on those wonderful years on our acreage in the middle of a German/Dutch community, and how they lovingly accepted this crazy Catholic city family.

About the Author

Anne Santin (pseudonym) was born in a large city on the prairies in Canada. Her life changed when her family moved from the comforts and conveniences of life in the city to the country. It was an adjustment from being able to walk to a store and pick up groceries with her mom in the city, to having to haul water to an underground cistern on the farm for household need. It was an adjustment of being able to have your weekly garbage picked up in the city, to learning how to recycle and conserve water on the farm.

The comfort and convenience of city life diminished and the love of country life took hold of Anne . An experience she will always cherish.

Printed in the United States
By Bookmasters